All About Animals
Otters

By Christina Wilsdon

Reader's Digest Young Families

Contents

Chapter 1
An Otter Story

The young river otter padded along a path by the stream. It was a special day. She was grown-up now—and it was the first day of being all on her own.

Just the day before, the otter had left her mother to find a new place to live. Her brother and sister had left home a few days earlier. Mama Otter was going to give birth to some new babies in a few months. So it was a good time for the young otter to mark out her own area along the stream.

She was not afraid to be on her own. She knew this land well. She had traveled over it many times with her family. There were many side trails that led down to the stream—and the young otter could find any one of them in a second. If she needed to escape from danger, she could just slide down a trail, slip into the water, and be gone. She knew every twist and turn in the stream too.

Best of all, she knew just the place that she would take over as her den. It was tucked under a log on top of the bank, right by the big curve in the stream.

Baby Business

Baby otters are called pups. A mother river otter usually has two or three pups at one time but can have as many as six. River otter pups are completely helpless. Their eyes do not open until they are four or five weeks old.

The stream and its banks were like a grocery store for the young otter. She had her pick of all kinds of food that otters like!

Most of the time, the otter caught small fish. She gobbled them up in the water. She even ate the bones! When the otter caught a big fish, she dragged it ashore. Sometimes she was full before she finished eating it. But she did not like leftovers. So she just left them by the stream. Small animals moved in quickly to finish the meal.

Sometimes the otter caught frogs, crayfish, and crabs. Once in a while, she even caught a mouse on land.

By the time winter arrived, snow formed a blanket over the land. Some animals curled up in their dens to sleep through the season. But the otter liked winter. On land, she bounded through the snow and then slid on her belly as if she were riding on a sled. She zipped down snowy banks into the water.

Swimming in cold water did not bother the otter either. She even liked to swim under ice! The water below the ice was warmer than the air above. Whenever she needed to take a breath, the otter simply poked her head up through a hole.

When she was tired, the otter crept through a tunnel in the bank of the stream that led right into her den. She curled up in a ball, flipped her tail over her nose, and slept soundly.

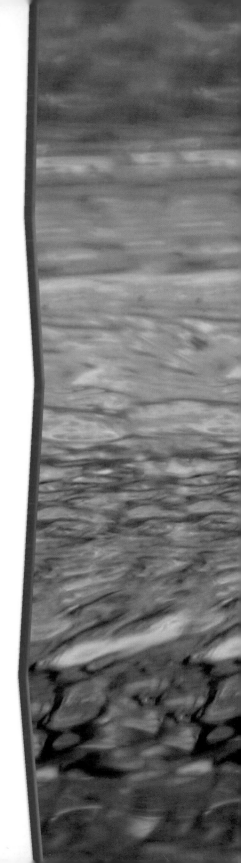

Den Doors

The river otter's den always has more than one entrance. At least one entrance leads directly underwater.

Most of the time, the otter spent her days alone. And that was fine with her. Sometimes she met another otter in the water. They would chase each other in the stream and play along the shore. Then the playmates would go their separate ways.

When the otter was about two years old, she was ready to find a mate. She knew that a male otter lived nearby. She smelled his scent along the trails near her den. The male otter knew where she lived too.

One day he slid down a snowy hill to greet her. They chirped at each other. Then they began to play. They zoomed down the snowy bank into the stream.

Splash! They landed in the water. Then they dove beneath its surface. Underwater, they swam in circles and twirled around each other. They did somersaults. They pretended to fight by nipping gently at each other's heads.

The otter and her mate spent almost a week together. Then the male otter headed off into the woods. Male river otters don't help raise their pups. So she would be alone again—at least until she gave birth to her first litter of pups in her warm, cozy den.

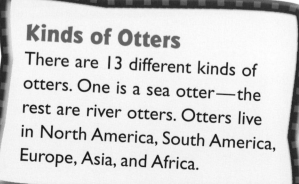

Kinds of Otters
There are 13 different kinds of otters. One is a sea otter—the rest are river otters. Otters live in North America, South America, Europe, Asia, and Africa.

Chapter 2
The Body of an Otter

When an otter swims with its head out
of the water, it dog-paddles with its feet.

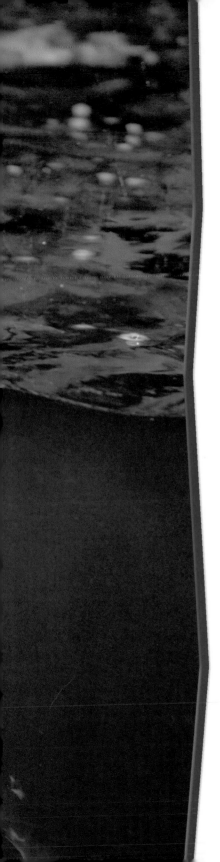

Long and Lean

An otter's body is shaped like a long hot dog. This sausage shape helps the otter glide easily through the water, like a fish. It also helps the otter slide through the tunnels that lead into and out of its den.

An otter's body is very flexible. An otter can bend backward and touch its nose with its tail! But an otter is more likely to use its tail to help support itself when it stands on its two hind legs.

Swimming and Walking

An otter is most at home in the water. In fact, a sea otter rarely leaves its home. Underwater, the otter swims by moving its whole body up and down while its hind legs push against the water. An otter easily swims at about 7 miles per hour. This is twice as fast as most people walk.

On land, a river otter walks on flat feet. When it runs, its long body seems to move like an inchworm's! Even though a running otter looks awkward, it can run faster than a person. It adds to its speed by sliding on patches of snow or mud.

Legs and Feet

All otters have short legs—but not all kinds of otters have the same kind of feet. The shape of an otter's feet is linked to where it lives and how it hunts.

River otters spend lots of time in water. Their feet are webbed, with thin skin stretching between the toes. Webbed feet are useful for paddling in the water.

The Asian short-clawed otter, however, has hardly any webbing on its front feet. This lets it move its toes freely to feel around in mud for crabs, snails, and crayfish.

A sea otter's feet are completely different from the feet of other otters. Its front feet look like they've been tucked into fuzzy socks. The toes are short, but they move easily to hold objects. The hind feet are webbed and look like flippers. They push strongly against the water as the sea otter swims.

Special Claws

Different kinds of otters have different kinds of claws. A river otter has strong claws that help it hang on to slippery fish. A sea otter is the only otter that can pull in its claws, like a cat.

A river otter catches large fish in the water with its mouth and takes it to shore to eat.

A sea otter has thicker fur than any other mammal. A spot on its back no bigger than a stamp may have about one million hairs on it! That's ten times thicker than the hair on a polar bear.

Otter Fur

An otter depends completely on its fur coat to keep it warm and dry in water. Unlike a seal, the otter does not have a thick layer of fat to help keep its body warm.

The otter's coat has two layers of hairs. One layer has long, thick hairs called guard hairs. Guard hairs work like a raincoat. They keep water out of the other layer, which is called the underfur.

An otter's underfur is very thick and fuzzy. Hairs in the underfur trap and hold on to air. This trapped air forms a blanket around the otter, holding in the otter's body heat.

Fur Care

An otter's fur must be kept very clean or it will not be able to trap air and keep the otter warm. So otters spend lots of time combing their fur with their teeth and claws. This is called grooming.

To dry their fur, river otters rub their bodies on plants and on the ground. Sea otters scrub their fur with their feet and use them to squeeze out water. Then they blow air into their fur to fluff it up!

Hearing and Sniffing

An otter's sense of hearing is excellent. Its ears are small and lie close to its head, which helps keep the otter's shape streamlined for gliding through water. An otter can close its ears to keep out water.

An otter's sense of smell is also excellent. It uses its nose to sniff for danger and to find out about other otters in the area. Otters leave scent marks wherever they go on land. Otters cannot sniff underwater. Their sense of smell is of no use there. They shut their nostrils to keep out water and use their eyes and whiskers instead.

Seeing

When out of the water, an otter cannot see as well as a human can. But an otter can see much better than you can underwater. An otter's eyes change shape slightly when it swims below the surface, which allows the otter to see clear images instead of blurry ones. However, an otter would need eyeglasses to see objects that are far away more clearly.

If the water is muddy or dimly lit, the otter must depend on its sense of touch. Its long, stiff whiskers can feel the vibrations of fish and other prey as they move through the water.

Many river otters live alone except in late winter, during the mating season. Some kinds of otters stay together for a year or so. Asian clawless otters mate for life.

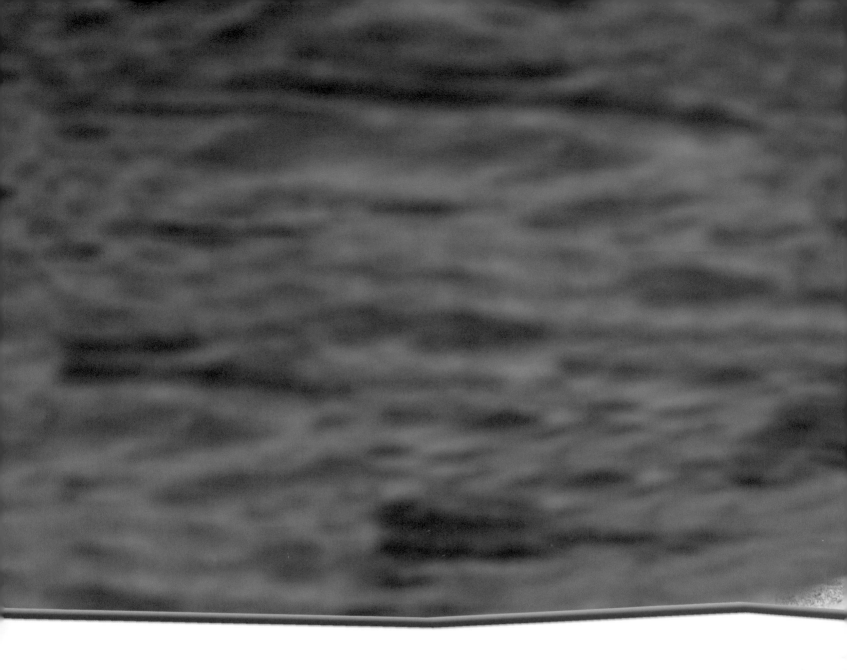

Chapter 3
Kinds of Otters

The northern river otter is the most common river otter in the United States and Canada. It lives in rivers, of course, and also lakes, ponds, marshes, and swamps.

River Otter

A river otter often swims just under the water's surface with only its head sticking out. If the otter senses danger, it will quickly slip underwater. A river otter can hold its breath underwater for up to four minutes.

A river otter catches slow-moving fish and eats them in the water if they are small. It drags larger fish to the shore to eat. River otters also eat frogs, turtles, insects, crabs, and crayfish. Sometimes, river otters eat ducks and muskrats—if they can catch them!

A river otter sleeps in a den that is in a riverbank or tucked under a nearby log or stone.

Eurasian Otter

The Eurasian otter is a river otter that lives in many parts of Europe and Asia and in some parts of northern Africa. It lives in more places in the world than any other kind of otter. It is sometimes called the European otter.

The Smallest Otter

The smallest otter is the Asian small-clawed otter. It is about 2 feet long and weighs up to 11 pounds—about as much as a big housecat. It lives in India, China, Indonesia, and a few other Asian countries.

Sea Otter

The sea otter lives the most watery life of all the otters. It rarely leaves the ocean. It can drink salty seawater, and the female even gives birth in the sea. But sea otters cannot stay underwater for more than a minute. They live in shallow water near the shore where they can dive to the sea floor for food.

The sea otter's body is covered with about 800 million hairs. That's about 8,000 times as many as you have on your head! These hairs form a thick coat that keeps the otter warm in the cold ocean. A sea otter spends hours each day grooming its fur to keep it clean and waterproof.

A sea otter paddles with its feet and tail while floating on its back. A sea otter eats and sleeps on its back, too. It often wraps a long piece of seaweed called kelp around its body so that it does not float off to sea while it naps!

Sea otters are one of the few animals that use tools. While on its back, a sea otter puts a stone on its chest and smashes clam shells against it to break them open. Sometimes an otter uses its stone to knock shellfish from rocks. The sea otter carries the stone in a pocket of skin under its arm!

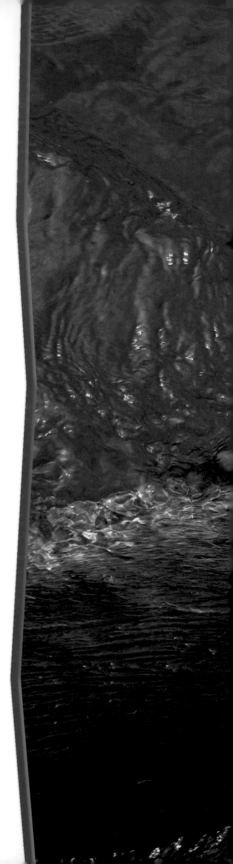

A sea otter spends most of its time floating on its back. Sea otters live in the Pacific Ocean along the coast of Canada and the United States.

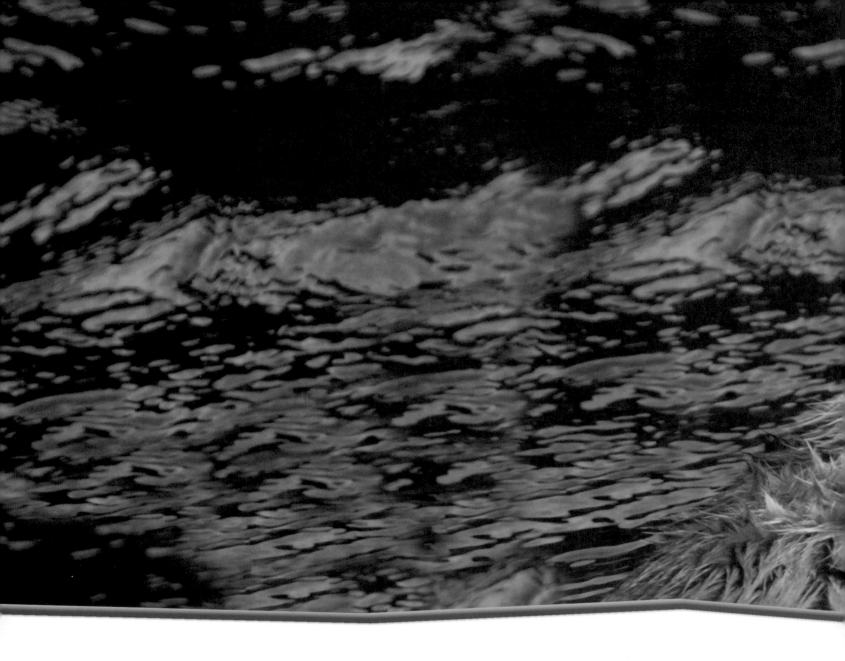

Chapter 4
Otter Life

A river otter sleeps in a den. River otters often use dens made by other animals, such as unused beaver lodges.

An Otter's Home

A river otter's home range includes all the places where the otter eats, drinks, and sleeps. It often overlaps with the home ranges of other otters. If there is plenty of food, otters don't mind feeding in the same area.

River otters do not try to keep other otters out of their home ranges, but they do protect parts of their home ranges. These protected areas are called territories. An otter that is defending its territory will attack other otters that enter it.

A river otter, for example, will chase intruders away from its den. Giant otters mark off and fiercely defend territories alongside rivers.

A river otter marks its territory by leaving scent messages. This is like putting up signs that say "Occupied." Other otters will usually find a different spot to use.

Otter Odors

To keep track of other otters in its neighborhood, a river otter depends on its sense of smell. It sniffs scent messages left by other river otters and leaves scent messages of its own for others to find.

A river otter uses its droppings to leave scent messages. The solid droppings are often left on easily seen spots, such as rocks, logs, and tufts of grass.

Otter Families

River otter pups are born in a den lined with soft grass, leaves, and fur. For the first few weeks of their lives, the pups drink their mother's milk. After the pups grow teeth, the mom brings them fish and other foods to eat.

River otter pups start learning to swim when they are about three months old. By this age, the pups' fluffy baby fur has been replaced by a waterproof coat. If the pups don't want to go in the water, their mom pushes them in!

The mother otter must teach her pups to hunt. She may do this by catching a fish, dragging it close to shore, and offering it to her pups. When the mom lets the fish wiggle away, the pups go after it.

The pups stay with their mom for up to one year. Then they are grown up enough to find homes of their own.

Some kinds of otters live in a big family group that has a mother, a father, and pups of different ages. A giant otter's family may have twenty otters. The older pups baby-sit the younger ones. All the otters help to protect the youngest pups. The whole family hunts together, but each otter chases its own meal. Giant otters work together as a team if they are attacked by predators, such as alligator-sized reptiles called caimans.

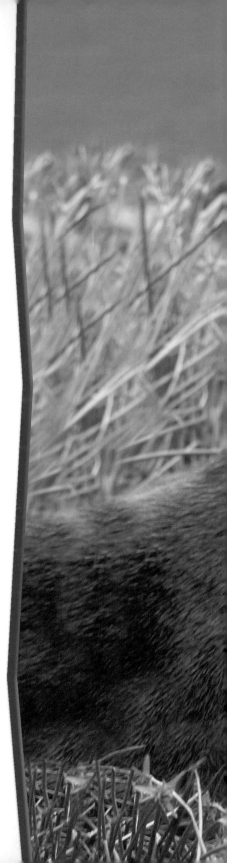

Most river otter families are made up of pups less than a year old and their mom.

Sometimes river otters slide on snow to get where they are going faster. Other times, sliding is just for fun!

Otter Fun

A group of otters is sometimes called a romp. This name comes from the otter's most famous behavior—romping, which means having fun. Otters in zoos and aquariums often attract crowds of visitors because they are so playful. Otters that are well-fed and have a safe place to live have time and energy left over for playing. They ripple through the water, leap, and dive. They swim up to the glass windows and look through them.

People who take care of sea otters give them things to play with so that the animals do not get bored. The sea otters are given tubes and balls stuffed with frozen shellfish. Sometimes seafood is frozen in chunks of ice. The sea otters eagerly chew and toss these "otter pops."

In the wild, otters chase each other and wrestle. River otters catch fish, let them go, and catch them again. They also toss pebbles and shells into the water, then dive after them.

In winter, river otters often slide on the snow on their bellies or backs. Sometimes the otters slide right down into the water! An otter starts its slide by bounding through the snow to speed up. Then it flops down and slides at speeds up to 18 miles an hour. That's faster than a human can run.

Chapter 5
Otters in the World

Sea otters stick their feet up out of the water to keep them warm.

Otters and People

Otters are among the world's most popular animals. Many people are charmed by their playful behavior. In the past, however, otters were often not liked because they ate fish that people could have eaten. As a result, people hunted otters just to get rid of them. In some places, a bounty was put on otters. This meant that a person would be rewarded with money for every otter killed.

Otters were also hunted for their fur. Using otter fur for clothing did not harm the population of otters hundreds of years ago. But when otter fur became popular in the mid-1800s, trappers began catching large numbers of otters. By the 1930s, river otters were almost extinct in most parts of the United States.

Sea otters were also nearly extinct because of hunting. Starting in the mid-1700s, fur traders from Russia, Europe, and the United States hunted sea otters for their thick fur. By the early 1900s, there were few sea otters left.

Protecting Otters

In 1911, the Fur Seal Treaty was signed by the United States, Russia, Japan, and Great Britain. It set rules to control the hunting of sea mammals. It also included laws to protect sea otters.

Since then, different nations have passed laws to protect other kinds of otters. In the United States, trapping river otters is limited by laws. In Brazil and other South American nations, giant otters are protected by law.

The Future of Otters

Otters are no longer hunted as they were in the past, but they still face threats to their survival. Pollution of rivers and seas is one threat. Loss of habitat is another. In South America, giant otters lose their homes when rain forests are cut down. Illegal hunting, called poaching, is also a problem.

Many people are working to help otters survive. One successful plan by scientists, otter organizations, and governments has been to transfer otters from areas with big otter populations to areas where otters used to live. Now these places are home to otters again. Many people think that's the way it "otter" be!

Fast Facts About Northern River Otters

Scientific name	*Lontra canadensis*
Class	Mammalia
Order	Carnivora
Size	From 35 to 51 inches long (males longer than females)
Weight	From 11 to 30 pounds (males heavier than females)
Life span	Up to 10 years in the wild Up to 21 years in captivity
Habitat	Rivers, streams, lakes, swamps, marshes

Young river otters can live
on their own when they
are about a year old.

Glossary of Wild Words

den   the place where a river otter sleeps, usually in a riverbank or under a log or stone close to the water's edge

freshwater   water that is not salty

grooming   cleaning fur, skin, or feathers by an animal

guard hairs   long, stiff hairs that make up the outer layer of an otter's fur coat. This layer keeps water away from the underfur.

habitat   the natural environment where an animal or plant lives

home range   the area where an otter eats and sleeps

mammal   an animal with a backbone and hair on its body that drinks milk from its mother when it is born

muskrat   a small, furry mammal that lives in rivers, ponds, marshes, and swamps

poaching	hunting that is against the law	**romping**	playing in a lively way
predator	an animal that hunts and eats other animals to survive	**territory**	the part of an otter's home range that is protected and defended by the otter
prey	animals that are hunted by other animals for food	**underfur**	the thick, woolly layer of fur close to an otter's skin. This layer traps air, helping to keep the otter warm.
pup	a baby otter	**webbing**	thin skin that stretches between the toes of some otters
raft	a group of sea otters		
romp	a group of otters		

Index